HOMECOMING

Joanna Ezekiel was born in Essex in 1969, and has worked as a teacher, bookseller and librarian. She is the author of four other books of poetry, including a full collection entitled *Centuries of Skin* published in 2010, and a first novel, *The Inside-Out House* (2014). She was the winner of the 2012 Rydale Poetry Competition and was shortlisted for the 2012 Bridport Prize. She is currently an Associate Lecturer in Creative Writing at the Open University, and lives in York. *Homecoming* is her second full collection. She has ridden on a camel twice, although not the same camel.

by the same author

CENTURIES OF SKIN
(Ragged Raven Press)

THE INSIDE-OUT HOUSE
(Indigo Dreams)

Homecoming

JOANNA EZEKIEL

Valley Press

First published in 2016 by Valley Press
Woodend, The Crescent, Scarborough, YO11 2PW
www.valleypressuk.com

First edition, first printing (April 2016)

ISBN 978-1-908853-65-3
Cat. no. VP0082

Printed and bound in Great Britain by
Charlesworth Press, Wakefield

www.valleypressuk.com/authors/joannaezekiel

Supported using public funding by
ARTS COUNCIL ENGLAND
LOTTERY FUNDED

Contents

Acknowledgements

In memory of my Dad, Danny Ezekiel: architect, town planner, conservation officer, DIY expert, citizen of the world.

Thanks to my partner Chris, for all his support; to the team at Valley Press; to everyone who has given me feedback, encouragement, and opportunities to publish these poems, or to read them to an audience; and to family, friends, and social media friends who have taken an interest in my writing and have spread the word.

These poems, or versions of them, have previously appeared elsewhere:

'Homecoming': Winner of the Ryedale Poetry Competition, 2012
'Wartime Wheatfield': *Sarasvati*
'Priceless': Shortlisted for the Bridport Prize, 2012
'A Score of Blackbirds,' 'Sunlight and Oranges,' 'Like a Holiday' and 'Malta': *Reach*
'Bridesmaid, Essex, 1976': *Obsessed with Pipework*
'Sari and Chapattis' and 'Dawn Poems': *The Mathmagician* (Leaf Books, 2013)
'The Wave': *Bolts of Silk*
'Tower Block, Syria': *Ink, Sweat & Tears*
'Jean Rhys Visits Par Beach': *Lapidus*
'No Flying Saucers': *Urban District Writer*
'The Rise and Fall of Passing Traffic': *Versions of the North: Contemporary Yorkshire Poetry* (Five Leaves, 2013)

Homecoming

I'll want my navy frock that sweeps the knee,
vermilion lipstick, brogues; today, you wait
in dishwater civvies, whistle, scuff gravel
at a corner baked with salt and rubble
where, underfoot, streets are thin gravy:
blood, energy, khaki have streaked into the sea.
When I read your telegram, I remembered
how caramel bubbles, then hardens.
Bittersoft edges burn my fingers.
Now I plunge through daylight's
sifted sugars, towards you: rinse out
the unwound clock, cobwebs,
simmering next-door-neighbours,
chicken bones that boil too soon.

Priceless

I used to cross-stitch with Roger Moore.
He'd pull up an embroidered chair,
avoid the gold chick, long-stitched,
upper right-hand side. Instead
he'd perch, all dress shirt and tux,
at the edge, with a wooden frame,
thread magenta, cinnamon, aqua.
I taught him blackwork, Algerian eye.
We'd speak of ex-wives, agents, teas;
Priceless, he'd mutter, skipping a stitch,
then start humming: always Shirley.
His favourite designs? Flowers,
back-filled English summers;
young Roger, one of the chaps,
chaining daisies on the sly.

Like a Holiday

Cacophony of Sunday traffic,
weather square and steady
for today, rain tomorrow, so
prams, dogs, short sleeves,
flip-flops, bikes
                    kids sitting
on a wall, arms swinging,
establishing their summer identity,
quick-changing.
                    Last night
Led Zeppelin on TV, 1972, bass riffs,
Robert Plant's quaver almost unearthly,
fuelled (I speculate) by unearthly drugs.
A man in a flat cap cycles past,
Plant's age about now,
how short our time has been.

Bridesmaid, Essex, 1976

In a pink blossom dress
I follow her satin dazzle.
She is marrying my cousin
who Mum says is the spit of Elvis
twenty years ago, not now.

Just beyond the canopy
Nan sits alone, no apron,
frowns at my swinging legs.
I imagine long grass swaying
in time to Hebrew rhythms.

From the children's table
I gaze at the square lawn
of dancefloor, sown with disco beats.
My little brother wears a bow tie.
We clap our hands.

Jean Rhys Visits Par Beach

The clayworks chimney
launches smoke –
does she watch
the slow unspiral
into one blank page?

Does the wind,
breathless as jazz,
goad her until
her improvisations
snap like reeds?

But how words bloom
as she comes across
an early dog-rose –
unexpected as a letter
from a friend.

Tower Block, Syria

bullet-hole windows
balconies tinged with grey
and the roof full of stones

sunrise spreads and behind
the sky booms and booms
a burnt block close by

smoke thickens to blue
it moves like a demon
tastes of mortar and blood

Sunlight and Oranges

for J.P. on her birthday

You tell me of your grandmother,
how she lived upstairs,

played patience and solitaire,
just like my grandmother,

living in a parallel room.
When I think of my grandmother's room

I think of a bowl of oranges,
a folding card table.

Sunlight at the window.
I would wish the same for yours,

my friend, who lives
with Jack on an island,

knits a purple cape,
grows pots of basil,

whose birthday it is. I hope
the upstairs rooms

of all your other birthdays
are singing for you today.

Mumbai Morning

This first morning
I rise early   my long crush
to absorb it all

sees me floating
at the hotel window
high above the pavement

The beach   an Indian flag   a man
hauls in his fishing line
ships   old   moored in the distance
remind me of my ancestors

once castaways along this shore
like lost Biblical passages
a Jewish thread that has me
flying over the Arabian sea

Could be coriander
growing in planters
by the red R2D2 postbox

and worn out by hard labour
a man lies on his thin mat
sleeps through sunshine that vies
with the yellow roofs of cars

This first morning
I running   on a Western track
keep an open mind   beyond
falling in love from the hotel floor

The Wave

Climate Change March, December 2009

for a while
the skies as blue
as our fingernails
and hats

below the placards,
scarves, banners
an undertow of anger
fuels us

we walk further
than expected – penance
for your new gloves
my bottle of water

at Parliament
we hear cheering
fall back
like birdsong

strange in December
upon Westminster Bridge
our blue concern
waves   at high tide

Wartime Wheatfield

*(after Evelyn Dunbar's painting Men Stooking
and Girls Learning to Stook, c.1943)*

The girls stand square
as hay bales, wait to fill sacks,
their muted green overalls
against the lime wheat.
The field is a stick of rock
with mint and wheat stripes
that taper to a point
under a cloudy sky
as far away as fresh potatoes,
corned beef pie, weak tea.
The men bend down, down,
reaching for grain,
instructing the girls who wear
pretty turbans of raw blue.

Women Picking Oakum in the Workhouse

Every day here is a sluice.
We bend our heads to ice-cold hours.

They call us parasites
while oakum thorns steal our blood,
paler than sunrise.

We cannot tell you that we dream
of being reborn with a kiss,

or of blood and oakum
seeding skeins of gold.

When we sleep, we're drowning
deep, deeper
than neon fish
or watercolour –

sometimes, a seaweed frond
names us,
then leaves us behind.

Richard III

He served as the warden at Carlisle Castle,
kept desperate Scottish folk
from townspeople who scratched a living.

Perhaps he felt his bones secreting ice
as night slivered into day
then out of it, scraping off the warmth.

Perhaps he amused himself
by flicking up his pocket knife,
surprising bare stone walls –

a white boar   a white rose
a childish animal face   bent legs
a maze of petals   curves and lines.

Perhaps he always was prepared to die
far from home: pictured his bones
curves and lines   under foreign ground.

What Riots

you're breaking up   I've sent you footage
yeah   that's me out front   ashes

empty shelves   my mate he's laughing
all these trainers made in China

it's over now   don't bother rushing in
you'll get no offers   nothing

what people giving up their homes
they should have seen that coming

how long we're staying?
you should know   you

voted us in

The Prime Minister's Garden

So George dashed down and we took a stroll,
as usual, through our salad halcyon days.
I trod some grass down with my sole,
then waited for its stupid puzzled rise
to batten it again but with my heel.
I had to yell a memo at the gardener:
These herbaceous borders are uneven.
Get them to conform ASAP.
We sniffed the lavender and champagne air, ours,
we looked towards the smoothest sky, ours,
we overheard the bloodless murmurs
of our neighbours: pleasant punctuation,
ours, then George said: 3.30?
Where's that lovely Hilda with the tea?

Grocer's Daughter

After homework she stands at the counter,
narrows her eyes till shoppers twist and jerk
around the aisles. She boxes them up
like Daz, Surf, Fairy, her favourite category
Homeowners. She knows which customers
take extra care when they deadhead roses,
dab at windows with chamois leather,
wax bathroom tiles, respectable
as Sundays. These will be her people
always. She pats her hair, hooks
the handles of a wire basket
over the crook of her arm.

Chicken

That time I finished rice and peas but pushed
chicken round my plate, desiring ice cream,

you blurted out (this was your last resort,
to call in from your past, that no-man's leap)

At your age I had just one egg a day.
Your scratch at time's too sharp for further words –

forty years, a continent away
where Hindu gods, not yours, still weep hot tears

that trickle down the corrugated slums
and splash into the Indian Ocean.

Sari and Chapattis

My mother remembers
our Dartford neighbour
showing her

how to make chapattis,
rolling the dough
between her palms.

One afternoon
in the school holidays
our neighbour brought over a sari,

wrapped the yards
of scarlet satin
around my six-year-old body.

I thought of summer,
of my mother's spice cupboard,
paprika and cinnamon.

I stood up straight
just like we'd practised in ballet
and tiptoed towards

the full-length mirror,
my neighbour's voice
cheerful behind me.

I stared at my half-Indian skin
brown against the red,
how it drank the brightness.

The sun kissing my reflection,
welcoming my shy twin
who'd vanish if I touched her,

drawing all my unknown questions
back across oceans
into a satin land.

Now I buy chapatti flour,
e-mail my mother the recipe,
roll the dough.

For Joseph David

my great-grandfather, who wrote Bollywood films

This book-lined room is backdrop
for your modest gaze. Photographed
without your Russian hat – Dad remembers
how you wore it through the heat and dust.
Did you take it off, close the shutters
at mid-day to write, could you hear

your audience applaud from market stalls,
rickshaws, your mind flickering
past the reels of languages you spoke,
the silhouettes of stories, waves of ragaas?
You wrote as if the silver screen
was big enough to hold a world

where your descendants would scatter –
England, Ahmedabad, Israel, Canada.

Julabies

I picture you, on his winning nights
as he upturns boxes of julabies

that curl like sticky heaps of question marks
asking for the chance of one of his smiles.

Shaken awake beneath a roulette moon
you join your mother, brothers, sisters, him

under the single kerosene lantern.
Your job to stay behind, clear up the crumbs.

I can only bring you small gifts each time:
an embroidered card for this, your birthday.

Take it: this is yours to keep forever.

A Score of Blackbirds

curved wings
bent heads

they lift off
from the cornfield –

each bird
a musical note

that resonates in the air
in the great hall of the air

Bus Shelter

IMOGEN
I am cold as a croft on the outside.
Inside, a fire, food in the pot
but nothing can get in.
No flowers no petals no dandelion clock
no Theo no wolf no rain.

PATIENCE
I think we just missed one. Yes, I saw it.
It slipped by the corner. Turned the corner
like a part of our lives flashed by with it.

IMOGEN
Sitting in class. Clock ticking.
I'll imagine my daughter crying, playing
on the swings with her Gran.
The music of her voice will flow to me like
water,
drown out the teacher.
And I'll remember to come home.

PATIENCE
On my hospital visit
I will look at the daffodils
while my sister talks, a lawnmower
rumbling on and on
with no regard for small grass.

IMOGEN
All these cars
by the light of the early morning sky.
Solidarity with lost souls.

PATIENCE
How the lampposts wink like diamonds
in the mine of the early morning sky.

IMOGEN   A lost animal, crying out of the dark.

AHMAD   This sky is full of moody blue thoughts,
              such as mine: but the sky brightens
              by degrees.

PATIENCE   My old, sweet memory, bearing
              snatches of song.

AHMAD   I'll tell them
              that I am growing to like English colours,
              the muted tones, not clear, not quite sludgy,
              subdued, like laughter
              heard through an oak door.

IMOGEN   I watched the babies in the park.
              They had open faces like sunflowers.

AHMAD   The scent of these daffodils haunts me
              with the temptation of spring.

IMOGEN   My mum won't understand.
              Settle down first, she'll say.
              What settled down must feel like:
              short white lines, straight and grainy
              by your side. People on bikes
              cycling in straight lines.
              The egg yolk yellow of bus poles
              solid on the speckled floor
              while the bus turns, stops, starts.

AHMAD   A jazz riff repeats
                 in my early morning head
                 like a siren.
                 The drone of a bass line
                 thuds in my chest.

PATIENCE   The daffodils will perk up their heads
                 and stare, deep as forests,
                 into the morning sun.

AHMAD   The shoes hurled towards George Bush
                 had traces of Iraqi earth on them.
                 Ploughed earth, blood stained earth
                 tearstained earth, windswept earth
                 indifferent earth he stood on, and shrugged.

IMOGEN   I dreamt I met Theo and his new girlfriend.
                 He had a black belt in karate.
                 His girlfriend went to get the drinks.
                 Theo and I sat there.
                 He started to smile at me.
                 How could I begin to explain?
                 'So, you can chop a brick in half,' I said.
                 I woke up. It was four a.m. And I knew.

PATIENCE   In my dream the birds at the back
                 leave quietly, flashing
                 their wild colours in the night.
                 I hear red steel drums playing
                 like dread wind. My aching limbs
                 speak to me of steel, long lost.

AHMAD   I dream of my homeland.
In the midst of it all is the river,
the hulled boats turned upward.
It is the ripple of the water,
the smoky traffic on the bridge.
It is the humid wind.
It is the solitary duck,
the quack of flying geese.
It is the midst and it is here, now.

PATIENCE   Some type of shooting star.
Long white tail and shorter tail.
And another. And another.
What are they, heading
into the silk gold of this sunrise?

Dawn Poems

1.

Finally, just the two of you
going through with it
in three a.m. shadows,

up in the attic, above
the laughter, guitar chords,
the careless slam of doors –

sounds that fall away
like a playground game
to the slow ringing
in your blood.

Afterwards you smoke,
swap small secrets,
sit side by side

travelling coolly
into pink dawn

as if you are already students,
independent –

and gossip, hassle, reputation

belong to square daylight
and safety in numbers.

2.

Once again, you sidestep
into someone else's night,
his good time,

you and he spinning out
blank hours
along the beige sofa,

you leave tobacco
constellations
on the coffee table

as gangster films
discard their soundtracks –
car brakes, shots

then, daylight layers
drawn curtains,

you remember home,
its green balcony,

your hands rest
on painted railings, edges blur

into a lavender sky
that whispers   start over.

Jane Queues with Lizzie Outside Betty's

Lizzie says the food is 'rather pukka
and service is totes Downton, worth the wait.'
Jane's nursed her hair into a Gibson Tuck
and wears her vintage blouse, the one Seb hates.
She hates him checking Facebook all the time.
Lizzie waves at Stonegate, at the bulb stalls.
Her voice soars with the cries of girls behind them
who bunch together clutching floral satchels.
St. Helen's Square roughshoes a lone guitarist
whose *Hallelujah*'s cheekily in tune.
Plump cakes on display line up for strangers.
Jane takes a selfie by the macaroons,
then bows politely at her realisation –
uploaded just in time for Seb's weight training.

Mary Has Been Invited Along to Make Up the Numbers

Shoegazing behind the other hens
all she has to do is take an arm
and hobble-stride the steps to *Revolution*

but she drank three Stellas on the train
then watched her peak glitter past the window.

Now her heels are techno beats on cobbles,
herds of lads are jiving in, too close

while Tudor second storeys loom like bouncers –
sharp monochrome, they've seen it all before.

Why can't she be home, where she'd be happy
to laugh at anti-social sitcom boys
and scold her cats for raving on the carpet?

Neon signs churn her to the bone.
She wonders who will notice if she's sick.

Mr and Mrs Bennet are in the Shambles

look   Mr Bennet   another yarn shop
alpaca bamboo   this season's shades

bluebell   pale cream
merge in the ramble of sky

but now   Mr Bennet   let us stop
in the midst of this road
to check our map

I hope the girls are watering the box hedges
you'd forget about order here

the way you can trace your path
through the market just by smell

salmon   espresso
roses lemon   chives

even you are talking today   Mr Bennet
your voice is bourbon with a hint of lime

No Flying Saucers

The friend I haven't seen for seven years
is out. Her scrawled note says
that she won't be in today.

I turn back through the quiet street
I know I've visited before
in other dreams,

which lie underneath
tonight's dream landscape
like a stack of photographs.

Crossing the main road, I find
the City buildings at the top
are smaller, friendlier than before.

No rollercoaster stretching overhead.
No maze of grey estates.
Instead, a sudden bus stop.

A Number Three passes me.
I know I'll have to wait another hour.
Strange to feel so sure here,

this road empty, for once,
of flying saucers.

Malta

is sunlight, luzzus
the come-hither red brick
of the casino

        is peeling white chip paint,
        bags of rubbish in the back street
        honking horns, barking dogs,
        drills everywhere

is the sea at high tide
in the bay, swooshing
over rocks, towards
benches where tourists
sit, mesmerised

        is a scrape of boy racers
        roaring into Paceville
        under trees filled
        with the gossip of birds is

                louder is
                Malta

Celebration

Somebody has set you down
here, in this one-off place
and you are on the road
with your dreams and your balloons
and your baskets of light.
And your heart is a truth, is a snail
inside its iced shell –
such wild icing today.

The Rise and Fall of Passing Traffic

is a wave that crashes and breaks
behind all my lives in houses.

A pane of double glazed glass
is all that stands between me
and the low sounds of engines.

At night, I hear intermittent waves
of traffic that sweep over me
like an old remembered lullaby,

until it ends and a door closes –
soft music, quiet conversation.

Even Though You Are Where You Love

and your past is a shining whirlpool
that you keep to remind yourself
of all you've left behind

some days you still hear
that voice whispering
'Off you go'

And you see yourself running
just for the loose speed of it
for the pulse of your heart
that keeps up, under a clear sky

for the springy grass
beneath your feet, the tilting fence
seen from the corner of your eye